THE
FESTIVE FOOD
OF
AMERICA

Martina Nicolls

ILLUSTRATED BY SALLY MALTBY

SERIES EDITOR: HENRIETTA GREEN

A Bulfinch Press Book
Little, Brown and Company
Boston • Toronto • London

Dedication
In memory of my mother

Copyright © 1991 by Martina Nicolls
Illustrations copyright © 1991 by Sally Maltby

First North American Edition

First published 1991 by
Kyle Cathie Limited
3 Vincent Square London SW1P 2LX
ISBN 0-8212-1883-2

Library of Congress Catalog Card Number
91-55273

Library of Congress Cataloging-in-Publication
information is available.

Bulfinch Press is an imprint and trademark of
Little, Brown and Company (Inc.)
Published simultaneously in Canada by
Little, Brown & Company (Canada) Limited

Designed by Geoff Hayes

PRINTED IN BELGIUM

Acknowledgements
For their help and support I would like to thank Jenny
Shaw, Debbie and Larry Freundlich, Avis Pelly, Anne
Armitage at the American Museum in Britain in Bath,
Claire Clifton, Janet Clarke and John Nicolls.

Contents

New Year's Day

It has been said that the South exists on 'hogs and hominy' and this is largely true. Southern pigs are big and fat and make good bacon, smoked hams and the old pioneer stand-by, salt pork. Hominy, one of the standard breakfast foods of the South, is dried corn kernels boiled in lye, hulled and left whole; 'grits' are ground hominy. Either can be boiled and served hot with butter, syrup or 'grease' (melted bacon fat) or cooled and then fried.

Cornmeal, finely ground dried corn, is versatile and used in both the delicate spoon breads of the Virginia gentry and the rough cracklin' breads and 'hoe cakes' of the countryside. Hoe cakes were made by the field hands on the plantations as they worked in the cotton rows; the workers mixed the cornmeal with hog lard, formed flat cakes from the mixture and slapped them onto their hoe blades to bake over an open fire.

Another traditional country way of baking corn bread is in a cast-iron skillet, which is a necessity in a Southern kitchen. This gives the bread a crisp bottom crust and a camp fire flavour. Serve it for a 'Good Luck' New Year's Day breakfast as all true Southerners do, hot, straight from the pan, with black-eyed peas and rice and a bowl of boiled turnip greens.

Hoppin' John

serves 6

This rather hearty dish of beans and rice most probably had its origins in the slave cabins of the South Carolina rice plantations that fringed the sweltering coastal marshes. It is, if you like, Soul Food, and as with many foods of humble beginnings it has now become a national treasure.

  Black-eyed peas are small, cream coloured beans with a black spot around the waist and a slightly smoky flavour. Southern cooks use salt pork but a good smoked bacon works as well.

225g/½lb/1cup black-eyed
  peas, soaked overnight
  in water
bay leaf
85g/3oz smoked streaky
  bacon in a piece, diced
1 medium onion, chopped
2 garlic cloves, minced
1 red chilli pepper
pinch of thyme
115g/4oz/½cup long-
  grain rice
salt and freshly ground
  pepper to taste

1 Drain the peas and put them in a deep pot with the bay leaf. Cover with about 2cm/1in cold water and bring to the boil. Simmer for 30 minutes.
2 Meanwhile, fry the bacon until crisp. Remove from the pan and fry the onion, garlic and chilli pepper until soft.
3 After the peas have simmered for 30 minutes, stir all the remaining ingredients into the pot, checking that there is enough liquid to cook the rice. Southern cooks do it by eye; there should be about 300ml/½pint/1¼cups, so add more water as necessary.
4 Cover and simmer gently for10–15 minutes or until the rice is cooked and the mixture is quite dry. If too much liquid remains, remove the lid and simmer for a minute or two to evaporate it.

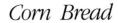

Corn Bread

serves 6

50g/2oz/¼cup bacon dripping or butter
140g/5oz/1cup yellow cornmeal
1 egg
85g/3oz/½cup plain flour
10ml/2teaspoons
baking powder
50ml/2fl oz/¼cup milk
50ml/2fl oz/¼cup water
pinch of salt

1 Melt the fat in a 23cm/9in skillet (cast-iron frying-pan).
2 Mix together the rest of the ingredients in a bowl, adding a little more water if necessary to make a smooth batter.
3 Pour the mixture into the hot skillet and bake in a preheated oven, 180°C/350°F/gas4, for 25–30 minutes or until golden on top and shrinking from the sides of the pan.

Mardi Gras

'Fat Tuesday', a literal translation of the French, is the day before Ash Wednesday. It is celebrated in many Catholic countries with carnivals and feasts before the Lenten fasts begin next day.

The fine old Creole city of New Orleans, on Louisiana's Gulf coast, has been famed for over a hundred years for its annual Mardi Gras celebrations. The day of revels, now less religious than it was originally, brings together the different elements that make the city one of the most exciting and interesting in America. It was the joint influences of the original Spanish settlers and the aristocratic French in the eighteenth century that gave the city its first identity. The architecture of the Vieux Carré (the old quarter) is rich: wrought iron balconies and porches, graceful façades and elegant courtyards. The inhabitants were the Creoles, keepers of an old tradition that gave New Orleans its fine food, and still does today.

The history of slavery in the South brought to New Orleans a legacy of African cultural mixes, producing some of the finest music in the world. It is the birthplace of the Blues and of Jazz, the home of Dixieland, the spiritual heartland of American Black music.

The flavour of Mardi Gras is intensified by the fervour of the music and the appetite of the revellers. Bands play through the night, everyone dances in masks. Street vendors sell local specialities such as oysters, deep-fried sweet pastries, Gumbos and tiny crabs.

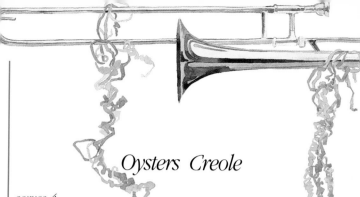

Oysters Creole

serves 4

During the carnival, street vendors sell these excellent bonnes-bouches, freshly fried, hot and crisp, to the revellers carousing the streets of New Orleans. Serve with lemon wedges and a piquante sauce.

24 large fresh oysters,
  shucked and drained
1 large egg
225ml/8fl oz/1cup milk
pinch of salt
freshly ground black pepper
pinch of cayenne

175g/6½oz/1cup fine
  dry breadcrumbs
85g/3oz/⅓cup butter
85ml/3fl oz/⅓cup
  olive oil
12 parsley sprigs
lemon wedges

1 Pat the oysters dry with paper towels.
2 Beat the egg, milk, salt, pepper and cayenne.
3 Spread the breadcrumbs on a plate. Dip the oysters, one by one, into the milk and then gently roll them in the breadcrumbs, patting them with your fingers.
4 Heat the butter and oil in a wide, deep frying-pan and drop in the oysters in a single layer. Cook for about 4–5 minutes, turning very carefully, until they are crispy and golden brown.
5 Remove and drain carefully on plenty of paper towels.
6 Keep the fat in the pan hot and drop in the parsley sprigs, fry quickly until very crisp but still green. Scatter over the hot oysters and serve at once with lemon wedges.

Gumbo

serves 6

One of the glories of Creole cuisine, Gumbo is a rich blend of fresh shellfish, onions, tiny okra and filé powder, herbs and hot pepper, all combining to great effect in a wonderful thick soup. The curious qualities of okra and filé powder give Gumbo a unique, slightly gluey consistency and sharp/sweet taste. Filé is said to have been manufactured originally by the Choctaw Indians from the tender young leaves of the sassafras tree, which were picked, dried in the sun and pulverized to a fine tilth for cooking and medicinal purposes. It is particular to Creole cooking, and is an acquired taste: use it with discretion.

Okra is plentiful throughout the Deep South. Before the introduction of filé powder, okra was the thickening ingredient used in soups and stews. No Gumbo is complete without it. In remote country areas where shellfish is hard to come by, a fine Gumbo is made with chicken, rabbit or squirrel. Sweet little crabs from the Mississippi Delta are used in New Orleans when in season and, traditionally, they would be cooked with okra rather than filé. Large prawns are excellent as well. Gumbo is substantial and needs few embellishments. Serve it in deep soup plates, spooned over a mound of fluffy white rice.

85g/3oz/½cup plain flour
140g/5oz/⅔cup unsalted butter
1 large Spanish onion, finely chopped
3 large tomatoes, skinned and chopped
450g/1lb okra, washed and sliced into 1.5cm/½in
   pieces
a few celery leaves, finely chopped
bay leaf
sprig of thyme
1 small red chilli pepper, seeds discarded
drop of Louisiana hot sauce (similar to Tabasco)
225ml/8fl oz bottle clam juice
1.5litres/2½pints/6¼cups fish stock
900g/2lb cooked prawns, shelled
2.5ml/½teaspoon filé powder (optional)
small bunch of parsley, finely chopped
salt and freshly ground pepper to taste

1 Spread the flour on a baking tray lined with foil.
Bake in a preheated oven, 180°C/350°F/gas4, stirring
occasionally for about 10 minutes or until pale nut
brown. Set aside.
2 Heat the butter in a large, deep saucepan. Add the
onion and tomatoes, stir briefly, then cover and cook
on a low heat for 5 minutes or until the onions are
transparent.
3 Add the okra, celery leaves, bay leaf, thyme and
chilli pepper and cook, stirring occasionally, for 3
minutes.
4 Sprinkle the vegetables with the browned flour.
Stir in the hot sauce, clam juice and fish stock.
Continue stirring over a medium heat until the
mixture is thick and smooth. Bring to the boil, reduce
heat and simmer for 10 minutes.
5 Add the prawns and cook gently for 20 minutes,
stirring occasionally.
6 Remove from the heat. Add salt and pepper to
taste. Stir in the filé powder and sprinkle with the
parsley.

George Washington's Birthday

As a lad, America's first President was questioned by his father about the chopping down of a favourite cherry tree. Young George, who could have denied all knowledge of this act of infamy, looked his parent straight in the eye and is said to have declared, 'I cannot tell a lie, Father, I cut down the cherry tree'. Having been, no doubt, suitably chastised, the future General and nation's first President was commended for telling the truth.

In Washington's honour, Cherry Cobbler is served every year on the third Monday in February. A delicious dessert, it has a flaky biscuit crust for the perfect golden-brown topping. Sour or sweet pitted cherries can be used, although the sour fruit has a truer flavour. To preserve cherries for the winter, little tart ones, much like Morellos, were usually sundried and strung on long threads hanging from beams in cool, dry attics; sweet cherries were bottled or made into jam.

George Washington's Birthday Cherry Cobbler

serves 6

Traditionally made with sour cherries for a sharp taste, Cobbler is usually served warm with vanilla ice cream.

140g/5oz/1cup self-raising flour
60ml/3½tablespoons/4tablespoons sugar
2.5ml/½teaspoon baking powder
pinch of salt
100ml/4fl oz/½cup double cream
50g/2oz/¼cup unsalted butter, melted
2 x 450g/1lb tins sour pitted cherries, drained, with
    75ml/3fl oz/⅓cup cherry juice reserved
20ml/1tablespoon/1½tablespoons arrowroot
drop of almond extract

1 Sift the flour, half the sugar, baking powder and the salt into a bowl. Stir in the cream, mixing well to form a soft dough.
2 Knead on a floured surface for 1 minute. Roll out to 1.5cm/½in thick and cut into six rounds of 6cm/2½in diameter. Dip each side in the melted butter and set aside.
3 Mix the cherry juice, remaining sugar, arrowroot and the almond extract in a bowl and stir until dissolved. Add the cherries and pour into 20x20x5cm/8x8x2in baking tin.
4 Place the rounds of dough, side by side, on top of the cherries. Bake in a preheated 200°C/400°F/gas6 oven for 20–25 minutes or until the top is golden and the cherries are bubbling.

St Patrick's Day

St Patrick's Day, March 17th, is a day of lively celebrations in Boston, New York and Chicago, where the considerable Irish populations have contributed to the character and prosperity of these great cities.

New York has a magnificent parade on Fifth Avenue with pipers, bands, and smiling Irish policemen. The whole city turns out to stamp and cheer and everyone wears a bit of the 'green'. The many lively Irish bars declare open house; these neighbourhood gathering places are well known for their friendly ambience and good plain food. Of course, on this particular day, there are always traditional Irish specialities chalked on the blackboard and a considerable amount of Irish stew, soda bread and boiled beef is consumed.

Carefully made, with a good cut of well cured meat, boiled beef is excellent eaten hot with mustard, horseradish and pickled beetroot as the traditional relishes. Leftovers can be cut into thin slices for sandwiches.

Mugs of full-strength Irish coffee are a warming and satisfying finish to a cold day's marching in the St Patrick's Day Parade.

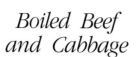

Boiled Beef and Cabbage

serves 8

1.8kg/4lb salt silverside or brisket of beef
1 large onion, peeled and stuck with 2 cloves
8 medium potatoes, scraped and quartered
8 medium carrots, scraped and quartered
1 small swede, peeled and cut into
   thick slices
900g/2lb green cabbage, cored
   and quartered
salt and freshly ground pepper

1 Soak the meat in cold water for a minimum of 2 hours, and drain.
2 Place the meat in a deep, lidded saucepan, add the onion and enough water to cover by 2cm/1in. Bring to the boil, skimming the scum and foam as it rises. Reduce the heat, partially cover and simmer for about 2½–3 hours or until the meat is tender.
3   Add the potatoes, carrots and swede and simmer uncovered for 20 minutes.
4 If there is enough room in the pan add the cabbage quarters, pressing them into the broth. Otherwise cook the cabbage separately in boiling salted water for about 15 minutes. Add salt and pepper to taste.
5 Remove the meat and vegetables and drain. Slice the beef and arrange on a platter in overlapping slices, surrounded by the vegetables. Serve the broth separately.

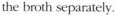

Sugaring-off

The North-eastern woods and the deep forests around the Great Lakes are sugar maple tree country. Between winter and spring, when it 'isn't too cold and it isn't too warm', the soft Sugar Snow falls, covering young daffodils with a thick, cool carpet. This signals the running of the maple sap, from which maple syrup is made.

In the good old days, before factories and refineries, the trees were tapped with hand-whittled wooden spouts; buckets were hung underneath to catch the thin sap, which was poured into iron cauldrons slung on stout poles between two trees. A crackling hot blaze was stoked through the night and willing neighbours and friends from miles around gathered to join the party and help stir the boiling sap, which had to be watched every minute until it began to thicken (waxing), at which point some of it was poured off into barrels and jugs to keep for syrup. Ladles of the hot liquid were drizzled onto plates of snow to make instant 'taffy' – a huge treat for everyone.

The remainder boiled on until it began to crystallize, when it was quickly transferred to pans to harden into crumbly dark maple sugar. It was a fine occasion for a dance and a local fiddler would play lively reels well into the night at the Sugaring-off party.

Maple Walnut Fudge

makes approx 25 squares

Pure maple syrup makes the richest fudge you can imagine. Make a fairly modest quantity, as a little goes quite a way. A sugar thermometer is a great help and it is probably wise to have one on hand.

500ml/16fl oz/2cups maple syrup
175ml/6fl oz/¾cup double cream
5ml/1teaspoon vanilla extract
115g/4oz/¾cup walnuts, coarsely chopped

1 Combine the maple syrup and the cream in a heavy saucepan. Stir over moderate heat until it begins to boil. Continue boiling, without stirring, until a teaspoon of the mixture forms a soft ball when dropped in cold water – 116°C/234°F on a sugar thermometer.
2 Remove at once from the heat and cool to lukewarm – 45°C/110°F – without stirring. Then beat the mixture until it thickens and loses its gloss.
3 Add the vanilla and nuts, and continue beating until creamy. Pour into a lightly buttered shallow tin, 20cm/8in square.
4 Leave to cool in the tin. Mark into squares before the fudge is completely cold.

A Quilting Bee

In spring, all over America, ladies gathered for Quilting Bees – days when they would work together assembling and finishing their quilts. It was also a splendid excuse for chattering and exchanging news after a long winter.

The 'pieced tops' or patchworks were stretched on to sturdy frames to be lined, backed and finely quilted before they could be used. A good quilter was famed for her matching of pattern and colour and, of course, the invisibility of her tiny stitches. In Mormon Utah, Quilting Sisters travelled to remote homesteads helping out with the quilting in exchange for room and board. No doubt they also brought longed-for company and gossip as well as quilting news.

Many quilts have been identified as coming from particular communities; Amish-Pennsylvania Dutch work is easily recognized by its plain geometric design and very bold use of colour, red in particular.

Quilting was a community affair, and hungry work. The industrious ladies would stop for light refreshment, home-baked cakes with perhaps some fresh buttermilk poured from cool earthen jugs. A lady, after all, was judged on the quality of her baking as critically as on the finesse of her quilting.

Quilter's Cake

In the 1880s, a Minnesota farmer's wife mentions in her diary tasting a brown sugar pound cake at a neighbour's Quilting. Whilst white sugar was expensive and difficult to come by, on most farms there would always be good milk, butter and eggs and, sometimes, a fine nut tree in the yard.

450g/1lb/4cups self raising flour
2.5ml/½teaspoon baking powder
large pinch salt
170g/6oz butter, softened
170g/6oz vegetable margarine
450g/1lb/2 cups light brown sugar
5 large eggs
250ml/⅓pint/1 cup milk
5ml/1 teaspoon vanilla extract
170g/6oz/1 cup walnuts (or pecans), chopped

1 Sift the flour, baking powder and salt. In an electric mixer cream the butter and margarine until light and add the brown sugar and beat until fluffy.
2 Beat in the eggs one at a time, and add the flour-mix alternating with the milk. Blend well and stir in the vanilla and nuts.
3 Pour into a well greased 25cm/10in tube tin or a 900g/2lb loaf tin and bake at 160°C/325°F/gas3 for 1½ hours or until the cake begins to shrink from the sides and the top springs back when lightly pressed. Leave in the tin for 20 minutes then turn out on to a wire rack to cool.

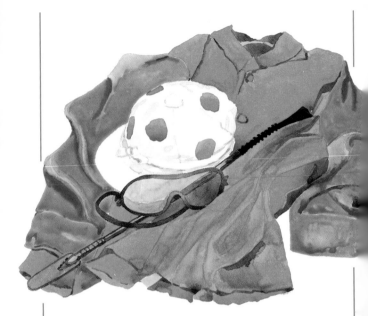

The Kentucky Derby

Since 1875 the first Saturday in May has seen sleek
three-year-old thoroughbred colts and fillies assemble
at Louisville's Churchill Down Racecourse for the
running of the Kentucky Derby, America's most
prestigious and famous race.

It is one of the great social events of the year, and
the even sleeker racegoers come from all over the
world. Traditionally the day begins early with elegant
breakfasts at the grandest homes and horse farms in
the county, where Kentucky cured hams baked to a
mahogany polish, tender, hot cream 'biscuits' and
Mint Juleps are served to start a glorious day of racing
and socialising.

Bourbon Baked Ham

serves 8

In Kentucky hams are smoked over hickory chips to give a delicate flavour to the meat. They are then glazed and baked to a crisp savoury-sweet finish and can be served hot or cold.

1.8kg/4lb smoked gammon joint
250ml/⅓pint/1cup Bourbon whiskey
115g/4oz/½cup dark, bitter marmalade
30ml/1½tablespoons/2tablespoons strong mustard

1 Place the gammon joint in the centre of a double piece of foil large enough to completely enclose the joint.
2 Mix the Bourbon, the marmalade and the mustard to make a glaze and spoon over the gammon. Wrap the meat in the foil to make a parcel, folding and pinching the edges tightly.
3 Bake in a preheated 190°C/375°F/gas5 oven for 1½ hours.
4 Remove from the oven (but do not turn it off). Carefully open the foil and allow the meat to cool for 5–10 minutes. With a sharp knife cut away the rind to leave a 1cm/½in layer of fat. Score the fat into squares and spoon the baked glaze over the surface, making sure the fat is well covered.
5 Leaving the foil open, return the gammon to the oven and continue cooking, basting frequently, for about 30 minutes or until the   glaze turns crisp and dark brown.
6 There will be plenty of gravy left from the glaze. Pour off as much fat as possible and serve the gravy separately.

Cream Biscuits

makes 12

No Derby breakfast is complete without a plate of hot buttered biscuits; light and flaky, they are an authentic American original. In the days of the old South, plantation cooks would beat the biscuit dough with a flat wooden mallet for half an hour to make them tender and light. Since the advent of baking powder in the late nineteenth century, biscuits are less violently and more quickly made, but just as excellent. Serve them straight from the oven, split in two and spread with honey-butter.

285g/10oz/2cups self-raising flour
5ml/1teaspoon salt
2.5ml/½teaspoon baking powder
30ml/1½tablespoons/2 tablespoons sugar
250ml/⅓pint/1cup double cream
115g/4oz/½cup unsalted butter, melted

1 Sift the dry ingredients into a bowl and stir in the cream, mixing well to form a soft dough.
2 Turn out and knead on a floured surface for about 1 minute. Gently roll the dough to 2cm/¾in thick and cut into 5cm/2in rounds.
3 Dip each side of the rounds in the melted butter and place on an ungreased baking sheet.
4 Bake in a preheated 200°C/400°F/gas6 oven for 15 minutes, until puffed and pale golden.

Honey-Butter

115g/4oz/½cup unsalted butter, softened
115g/4fl oz/⅓cup thick honey
5ml/1teaspoon grated orange rind

1 Beat all the ingredients together until fluffy

Mint Julep

serves 1

Kentucky is famous for the 'blue grass' that feeds its horses and for the Bourbon whiskey that cools its civilized palates. Mint Julep, mixed with ice made with 'branch' (spring) water, is the classic Southern drink for hot, relaxed days.

Keep the tumblers in the freezer until they are frosted and opaque.

5ml/1teaspoon sugar
6–8 fresh mint leaves
115g/4oz/½cup crushed ice
85ml/3fl oz Kentucky Bourbon

1 Crush the sugar and mint leaves in a glass and stir in some of the ice.
2 Mix in the Bourbon.
3 Pour the mixture into a frosted tumbler and fill to the brim with the remaining ice. Decorate with a mint leaf or two.

Fourth of July Picnic

July 4th, Independence Day, commemorates the adoption by the Continental Congress of the Declaration of Independence in 1776. This document gave the American people the right of government by choice, and the resulting hard-fought Revolutionary war between England and Colonial America consolidated this freedom. Picnics, fireworks, rodeos and even log-pulling races are part of the nationwide celebrations. Every village and town puts out flags and cranks up the band. Farmers in the rich Midwest farm country of central Indiana still think a Fourth of July Picnic without Fried Chicken, Lemonade and Grandma's Cream Pie would be unconstitutional.

Fried Chicken

serves 6
Serve fried chicken cold and eat it with your fingers, plain and unadorned but for a sharp mayonnaise and salt and pepper.

1.8kg/4lb free-range
   chicken, jointed
1 egg, beaten
juice of 1 lemon
300ml/½pint/1¼cups milk
115g/4oz/¾cup plain flour

paprika to taste
sunflower oil, for frying
bay leaf
salt and freshly ground
   black pepper

1 Put the chicken pieces in a bowl. Beat the egg with the lemon juice and milk and pour over the chicken. Marinate for 30 minutes.
2 Meanwhile, mix the flour, salt, pepper and the paprika in a sturdy paper bag. Drain the chicken, put a few pieces at a time in the paper bag, hold the edges firmly together and shake well to coat the chicken. Continue with the remaining pieces.

3 Heat about 2.5cm/1in oil in a wide, heavy frying-pan. When hot but not smoking, add the bay leaf and chicken pieces, skin side down, and fry over a medium heat until golden and firm. Turn with tongs and brown the other side.

4 Lower the heat and fry for about 20 minutes, turning once more, until the chicken is cooked through, golden brown and crusty.

5 Drain on crumpled paper towels and leave to cool.

Indiana Cream Pie

serves 6

A rich, satin-smooth pie which is heavenly topped with sliced fresh peaches or blueberries.

170g/6oz shortcrust pastry
115g/4oz/½cup unsalted butter
85g/3oz/⅓cup sugar
500ml/16fl oz/2cups double cream
30ml/1½tablespoons/2tablespoons cornflour
2.5ml/½teaspoon vanilla extract
grated nutmeg

1 Roll out the pastry to 5mm/¼in thick and line a 21cm/8in flan tin. Cover the base with a piece of kitchen foil, fill with dried beans and bake blind in a preheated 200°C/400°F/gas 6 oven for 15 minutes. Reduce the heat to 180°C/350°F/gas4, remove the beans and foil and bake for a further 20 minutes, until golden brown.

2 Melt the butter with the sugar and 400ml/⅔pint/1¾cups of the cream in a double boiler.

3 Mix the cornflour with the remaining cream and vanilla, stir into the hot cream and cook gently, whisking constantly, for 2–3 minutes until very thick.

4 Pour filling into the pie shell, grate nutmeg over the top and bake in a preheated 200°C/400°F/gas6 oven for 5 minutes. Cool on a rack and serve cold.

Shaker Strawberry Feast

The Shakers were disciples of Mother Ann Lee, an English immigrant to America in 1774, who was regarded by her thousands of followers as the female reincarnation of Christ. The Shakers, an off-shoot of the Quaker sect, established their first communities in the late eighteenth century. They took their name from the religious ceremony in which they danced, 'shaking out' their sins and refreshing their spirits. The rules were austere: a shunning of artifice and embellishment, common ownership of goods and, it must be said, equal rights for women. These flourishing and self-sufficient communities lived a celibate life and relied entirely on converts - not surprisingly they are now virtually extinct.

Communities, such as Hancock in Massechusetts were primarily agricultural, although the Brothers and Sisters made and sold household implements, farm tools and furniture of simple, uncluttered functional design and excellent workmanship.

For all that the Shakers were in many ways austere, their food was rich with the abundant crops of fruit and vegetables. They were noted for their hospitality to travellers and those fallen on evil times.

The Hancock Shaker Village is now a museum. Old diaries and letters mention the celebration of an annual strawberry shortcake meal. It was prepared at the peak of the picking season in mid-July, when quantities of this delicious dessert were consumed with great delight.

Strawberry Shortcake

serves 6

225g/8oz/2cups plain flour
20ml/1tablespoon/1½tablespoons sugar
15ml/3teaspoons baking powder
pinch of salt
115g/4oz/½cup butter
175ml/6fl oz/¾cup milk
575ml/1pint/2½cups double cream, whipped
675g/1½lb strawberries

1 Sift the flour, sugar, baking powder and salt into a bowl. Add 85g/3oz/⅓ of the cup butter, rubbing it in with your fingers to a fine crumble.
2 Add the milk and mix it lightly with a fork to make a soft dough.
3 Roll out the dough onto a floured surface to 1cm/ ½in thick. Cut into 6 rounds with an 8cm/3in cutter.
4 Transfer to a lightly greased baking sheet. Melt the remaining butter and brush the rounds lightly. Bake in a preheated 220°C/425°F/gas7 oven for 12 minutes or until crusty brown.
5 To serve: split the hot shortcakes in two and brush with melted butter. Place half a shortcake on a plate, top with strawberries and a big spoonful of the cream. Cover with the other shortcake half, and decorate with more strawberries and whipped cream.

Gilroy Garlic Festival

In California's fertile heartland lies Gilroy, the fragrant centre of the state's garlic growing and processing industry. Aside from the massive quantities of the 'scented pearl', California grows marvellous vegetables and fruit such as avocados, citrus and soft fruits and has, through the good works of the many restaurateurs and chefs, spearheaded the revolution in American cuisine. The climate varies from desert to cool forest with the rolling hills of the Napa and Sonoma valleys to the north of San Francisco, producing some of the finest wines in the world. These elements combine to make California a place of gastronomic pilgrimage for Americans and Europeans alike – the food is fresh and light, the produce local and the blending of flavours and ingredients reflects the many cultural influences of the American West. American cooking has taken on a new spirit and direction under the Californian sun.

Twelve years ago the town of Gilroy declared a festival to pay homage to garlic. This aromatic three-day event is a veritable extravaganza with every possible use and adjunct of garlic being displayed. It was here, apparently, that garlic ice cream was first invented. And it is here that one

can buy anything and everything to do with garlic.
The air is thick with the pungent aroma – Will
Rogers, the home-spun American humorist, described
Gilroy as 'the only town in America where you can
marinate a steak by hanging it on the clothes line'.

Avocado Garlic Soup

serves 6

This delicate cold
soup is best made
with fresh young garlic
and ripe but firm
avocados. In
California
avocado
trees
grow in
abundance and many a
back-yard will have its own
proud tree dripping with fruit. The young purple-
green garlic is almost sweet with a sharp edge that
does not offend the mellow avocado. Fresh juicy
limes are also plentiful in California and can be
picked off the tree outside the back door. Serve in
small white porcelain bowls.

1litre/1¾pints/4½cups chicken stock, degreased
4 fresh young garlic cloves, peeled and chopped
2 medium avocados, skinned and diced
juice of 1 lime
salt and freshly ground pepper
fresh coriander leaves to garnish

1 Combine all the ingredients and blend in a
liquidizer, in batches, until satin smooth.
2 Adjust the seasoning to taste. Chill for at least two
hours. Pour into individual soup bowls and decorate
with coriander leaves.

Indian Artists' Market

Santa Fe, New Mexico, is Spain's old Colonial capital. Founded in 1610, it is a timeless and mellow place, where the sun is bright and hot and the air cooled by mountain breezes. Fiestas and markets take place throughout the year with the Indian Artists' Market in mid-August as one of the most colorful and popular art fairs of the summer.

More than 500 of the South-West's American-Indian artists bring their work to be judged in competitions and sold in a lively street market. It packs the city's tree-lined square and twisting adobe streets. The quality and variety of the hand-woven rugs and baskets, traditional pottery, kachina dolls, drums and astonishing sand paintings are shown in the number of buyers who flood the streets from dawn onwards. During the day there are feasts of specially prepared Indian foods and stalls selling wonderful spicy-hot snacks of Indian fry bread and hot chilli sauce. The food in Santa Fe strongly reflects the two cultures that have influenced the South-West – Indian and Spanish; and the ingredients – corn, squashes, chilli peppers, pumpkin, pinon nuts and beans – are all native to the land.

Indian Fry Bread

makes about 20

Fry Bread is an Indian staple. Easy to make, the fried rounds of bread are crisp and golden on the outside and light and soft within. They are delicious split open and served warm with butter and wild honey. For picnics eat them cold sandwiched together with cream cheese and chopped fresh chives, or with a sharp chilli sauce (see page 36).

225g/8oz/2cups self raising flour
7.5ml/1¼teaspoons baking powder
pinch of salt
20ml/1tablespoon/1½tablespoons olive oil
250ml/⅓pint/1cup warm water
sunflower oil for frying

1 Sift the flour, baking powder and salt.
2 Pour in the oil and water and mix to a soft dough.
3 Knead on a floured surface for about a minute. Pat into a 1cm/½in thick round and set aside, covered, for 20 minutes.
4 Shape into balls about the size of an egg. Pat flat and poke a hole through the centre with your finger.
5 Heat 5cm/2in of sunflower oil in a deep, medium-sized saucepan until hazy. Fry the dough in batches, four or five at a time, for about 5 minutes, turning often, until golden brown.
6 Remove with a slotted spoon and drain on paper towels.

Chilli Sauce

(enough for 20 Indian Fry Breads)
The variety of chilli peppers is
wondrous. Green, red and
orange, they can be fiery,
unbelievably fiery, or
even sweet and mild.
Individually, red and green
chillies are made into sauces to
be served 'on the side' with
virtually all meats, grains and beans.
If you prefer your chilli sauce over
the food ask for it to be served 'like Christmas' with
the red and green sauce dolloped side by side on the
top.

This fresh chilli sauce can be served hot or cold
and is particularly good as a topping for cornbread or
vegetable bakes. If you have the digestion of a cast-
iron boiler, double the quantity of chillies and do not
discard the seeds.

40ml/2tablespoons/2½tablespoons olive oil
5–6 fresh green chilli peppers, either hot or mild,
    deseeded and finely chopped
1 medium onion, finely chopped
2 large tomatoes, finely chopped
2 garlic cloves, minced
20ml/1tablespoon/1½tablespoons cider vinegar
salt

1 Heat the oil in a frying-pan and add the chillies,
onion, tomatoes, garlic and vinegar.
2 Sauté the mixture until the liquid has evaporated
and the vegetables are just tender. Add salt to taste.

Corn and Cheese Pudding

serves 6

A Navajo savoury pudding similar to corn bread but richer and substantial enough for a light luncheon or supper dish. Serve it hot, cut into thick slices, topped with a fiery chilli sauce (see page 36).

350g/12oz tin corn kernels, rinsed and drained
175ml/6fl oz/¾cup milk
225g/8oz/1½cups yellow cornmeal
75ml/5tablespoons/⅓cup olive oil
2.5ml/½teaspoon baking powder
2 large eggs, well beaten
¼teaspoon salt
3 fresh green chillies, deseeded and chopped
100g/3½oz/1cup Cheddar cheese, grated

1 In a large bowl mix the corn and milk. Add the cornmeal and olive oil and stir well.
2 Stir in the baking powder, eggs and salt. Mix in the chillies and cheese.
3 Pour into a greased, deep glazed earthenware baking dish and bake in a preheated oven, 200°C/400°F/gas6, for about 35 minutes or until slightly browned on top and a knife inserted in the centre comes out clean.

Hatch Chilli Festival

Chillies are New Mexico's biggest cash crop and Hatch is the state's chilli-growing capital. Every year on Labor Day an annual chilli festival is held in the hangar at the local airport, and this jolly occasion celebrates every conceivable use of the ubiquitous vegetable, with cookery competitions, carnival rides, cook-outs and barbecues and the crowning of the Chilli Queen. Everyone wears Western hats and cowboy boots and avidly discusses the best way to make chilli con or without carne. This is a cause of great rivalry between states, with Texans declaring theirs to be the best – a statement disputed by everyone else in the South-west.

The one fact generally accepted is that beans are *not* cooked with chillies and meat. Beans are served on the side and 'that is that' said a Texan friend. Only Easterners or, worse still, Californians, would think of messing up a good Bowl of Red. After that it is up to you to decide if you prefer chillies fresh or dried, prepared chilli powder or home-made, minced meat or finely chopped beef or pork or even whether or not to add tomatoes – just don't add beans!

Chilli con Carne

serves 6

What we know as Chilli con Carne is a development of a Native American tribe stew of hot peppers and vegetables. Nowadays incorporating meat, a bowl of red, as it is called in the South-west, is basic, beautiful and either fiery or mellow.

Cook the chilli the day before you want to serve it, as it improves with reheating. Serve in deep bowls with, for those who insist on fancy trimmings, some finely chopped onion, grated Cheddar and sour cream to stir into the brew.

30ml/1½tablespoons/2tablespoons
   olive oil
1 medium onion, finely chopped
2 garlic cloves, minced
6–8 fresh green chilli peppers,
   deseeded and cut into thin strips
200g/2lb stewing beef or pork,
   diced
20ml/1tablespoon/1½tablespoons
   plain flour
20–30ml/1–1½tablespoons/
   1½–2tablespoons
   chilli powder,
   according to taste
5ml/1teaspoon ground cumin
3 large tomatoes,
   chopped
water
small bunch fresh
   coriander, finely chopped
salt and freshly ground pepper

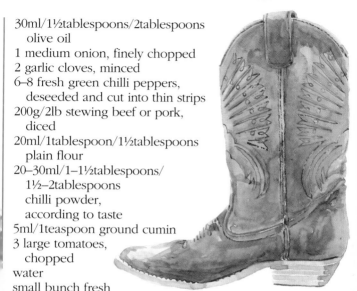

1 Heat the oil in a heavy casserole, and add the
onion, garlic and chilli peppers. Sauté gently until
softened.
2 Remove the vegetables from the pot, add the meat
and brown it well. Add the flour and stir to coat the
meat. Add the chilli powder and cumin and cook for
a minute or two, stirring constantly.
3 Stir in the tomatoes and onion-chilli mixture. Pour
in enough water to just cover the meat. Bring to the
boil, then cover and simmer very slowly for about
2½–3 hours or until the sauce has reduced and
thickened, the vegetables have almost disintegrated
and the meat is very tender. Season with salt and
pepper and sprinkle over the coriander.

Labor Day

The first Monday in September, Labor Day, is a national holiday, honouring all the workers of America. It is the American version of the European May Day, without the anthropological associations. Traditionally this is the last day of the summer holidays, before going back to work and back to school, and it is celebrated all over the country, with picnics, country fairs, barbecues and bake-outs.

In true North-east Yankee fashion, the people of Bridgehampton, a seaside summer retreat for New York's literati, send off the summer with a Clam and Lobster Bake. Long trestles are set in the shade of old oaks, chilled jugs of the local excellent Chardonnay are in plentiful supply and steamed shellfish are heaped on large platters with melted butter and lemon juice.

It is wonderfully messy and sublime eating. Though purists insist this should take place on the beach, ideally at twilight with sea-water-filled cauldrons and fires of driftwood, a Clam and Lobster Bake can taste just as wonderful in a summer garden.

Clam and Lobster Bake

serves 6
This impressive dish is made by building up alternate layers of ingredients and fresh seaweed. Don't worry if clams are not available; it will be equally good without them.

Take an enormous stew pot, about 9litre/2gallon capacity, and, using plenty of very fresh seaweed, proceed thus in layers: cover the bottom of the pot with seaweed, lay on top 4 Quahog clams (very large molluscs), used for flavouring the broth, add another layer of seaweed and cover with 6 scrubbed baking potatoes left whole. Then add another layer of seaweed, 6 chicken quarters, more seaweed, 6 sweet corn in the husks with the silk carefully extracted, even more seaweed,1kg/2.2lb live littleneck clams, washed and de-sanded, a final layer of seaweed and, to finish off the pot, 6 x 675g/1½lb live lobsters.

Pour about 575ml/1pint/2½cups fresh water into the pot. Cover tightly and steam over medium heat for 45–60 minutes. Remove the lobsters to a platter, and keep warm. Cook the rest a further 20 minutes or until the chicken and potatoes are tender.

Discard the Quahogs and the seaweed and pile everything else onto separate platters. Provide crackers for the lobsters, plenty of lemon wedges, melted butter to dip the food into and piles of paper towels to tuck under chins.

Blueberry Cake

serves 6

Blueberries are a native fruit in the United States, originally found growing in the scrubby, sandy soil around the North-east coast from July through to mid-September. Now they are cultivated commercially to satisfy the almost infinite American appetite for blueberry desserts, muffins and cakes. This good, moist cake with a crumble topping is an essential finish for a Clam and Lobster Bake.

150g/6oz/1cup self-raising flour
50g/2oz/¼cup sugar
pinch of salt
2 large egg yolks
50ml/2fl oz/¼ cup milk
50g/2oz/2tablespoons unsalted butter, melted
175g/6oz/1cup blueberries
squeeze of lemon juice

Crumb Topping
25g/1oz/2tablespoons sugar
25g/1oz/¼cup plain flour
25g/1oz/1tablespoon butter
pinch of cinnamon

1 Sift the flour, sugar and salt into a bowl. Stir in the egg yolks, milk and melted butter. Beat vigorously until blended.

2 Line a 20cm/8in square cake tin with baking parchment and grease it thoroughly. Spread the mixture evenly, scatter the blueberries over the top and add a squeeze of lemon juice.

3 To make the crumb topping, combine the sugar, flour, butter and cinnamon and work into a fine crumble with your fingers. Sprinkle evenly over the blueberries.

4 Bake in a preheated oven, 180°C/ 350°F/gas4, for 30 minutes or until a knife inserted into the centre of the cake comes out clean. Serve warm with vanilla ice cream.

Festival of San Gennaro

The patron Saint of Naples travelled quite happily to the streets of Little Italy in New York where he is as revered as in the noisy alleys of his home town. San Gennaro came to New York with the Neapolitans who settled in the prosperous New World towards the turn of the last century. But his history goes further back, to the waning days of the Roman Empire, under the desperate reign of the Emperor Diocletian. San Gennaro, then a Bishop in the early and much-persecuted Christian Church, was tormented and martyred for his beliefs. His remains were gathered by devout followers and brought to Naples where they caused many miracles over the centuries. A relic of the revered saint is carried in procession through the streets of Little Italy as it has been in Naples since time immemorial.

In the ten-day Feast period, mid-September the entire neighbourhood turns out to celebrate with food, music, religious processions and solemn Masses. The excellent restaurants, coffee houses and shops put up decorations, set tables and stalls in the street, and a fine time is had by all. One of the great inventions of the local Italian delis (and now a national by-word for over-indulgence) is the hero sandwich. It needs an appetite of heroic proportions to eat one. Basically a very long French loaf is split and filled thickly with any combination of Italian salamis, salad, spicy sausage, tomatoes or tomato sauce, meatballs, fried peppers and Mozzarella or sharp Provolone cheese, or whatever you fancy. A hero can be ordered up to 130cm/4ft in length and could feed a small army.

Hero Sandwich

serves 2–4
30cm/12in French loaf, split horizontally
40ml/2tablespoons/2½tablespoons olive oil
2 large tomatoes, thinly sliced
115g/4oz Mozzarella, thinly sliced
50g/2oz Italian salami, thinly sliced
1 large red pepper, seeded and cut into strips
50g/2oz prosciutto, thinly sliced
50g/2oz sun-dried tomatoes in oil, drained
a few fresh basil leaves
a few capers
freshly ground black pepper

1 Lay the split halves side by side. Drizzle the olive oil evenly along the cut surface of both halves and season with pepper to taste.
2 Layer the remaining ingredients in the order listed along the bottom half of the loaf. Top with the other half and firmly but gently press on to the filling, being careful not to squeeze it out the sides.
3 Cut into four thick slices and eat at once or wrap in foil and chill until needed.

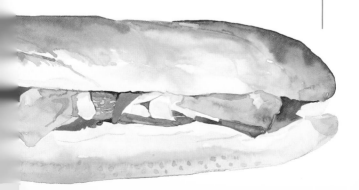

Harvest Supper

On the South Dakota prairies, The Harvest Supper was an annual event for homesteaders who attended church for a rousing sermon, to give thanks for the harvest and enjoy the hearty frontier fare contributed by the ladies of the county.

Pheasant Bake

serves 10
4 pheasants
6 thick slices of brown bread, toasted
150g/5½oz/⅔cup butter
1 medium onion, chopped
2 stalks of celery, finely chopped
115g/4oz mushrooms, finely sliced
2 sage leaves, crumbled
575ml/1pint/2½cups chicken stock
50g/2oz/¼cup flour
sprig of thyme
250ml/⅓pint/1cup single cream
90g/3½oz/1cup fresh breadcrumbs
salt and freshly ground pepper to taste

1 Roast the pheasants in a 200°C/400°F/gas6 oven for 45 minutes. Strip off the flesh and chop roughly.
2 Crumble the toast into a bowl and set aside. Heat 50g/2oz/¼cup of the butter in a frying-pan and sauté the onion, celery and mushrooms until tender. Add the sage, season and remove from the heat.
3 Pour half the chicken stock onto the crumbled toast, stir in the vegetables and leave for about 10 minutes. Spread the mixture in the bottom of a buttered, deep ovenproof dish and arrange the pheasant pieces on top.

4   Melt the remaining butter and blend in 50g/2oz/
¼cup of the flour with the thyme. Cook gently, stirring
constantly until pale golden. Add the remaining
chicken stock and the cream and whisk over medium
heat until thick and smooth. Season.
5 Pour the sauce over the pheasant and vegetables,
scatter the breadcrumbs on top and drizzle with the
remaining melted butter. Bake in a preheated 180°C/
350°F/gas4 oven. Serve piping hot.

Vinegar Pie

serves 6

Pioneer families travelled West with a good
supply of sturdy vinegar barrels.
Vinegar   was used for cleaning pots, as
a mild antiseptic, a   preservative of foods and
as a substitute for lemons, scarce as hens' teeth.

170g/6oz shortcrust pastry
225g/8oz/1cup sugar
50ml/3tablespoons/
¼cup plain flour
pinch of ground mace
pinch of cinnamon
175ml/6fl oz/¾cup water
30ml/1½tablespoons/2tablespoons cider vinegar
75g/2½oz/⅓cup butter, melted
2 large eggs, beaten

1 Roll out the pastry on a lightly floured surface to
5mm¼in thick and line a 21cm/8in flan tin. Prick the
bottom with a fork and bake blind in a preheated
190°C/375°F/gas5 oven for 15 minutes. Turn down
the oven to 180°C/350°F/gas4.
2 Mix the sugar, flour and spices in a bowl. Stir in
the water, vinegar and butter and beat in the eggs.
3 Pour the mixture into the pie shell and bake for
30–35 minutes until puffed and golden.
4 The filling will settle as it cools; slice when cold.

Halloween

October 31st, All Hallows' Eve, is the night witches fly on broomsticks across the moonlit sky, Jack-o-Lanterns, with their grinning faces carved in a variety of expressions, flicker mysteriously in dark windows and children all over America dress in spooky costumes and frightening masks. They go from house to house asking for 'Trick or Treat' – a custom evolving from pagan Celtic fire festivals to frighten away evil spirits and souls returning from the dead, and to appease the supernatural powers whose sinister influence controlled the forces of nature. These pagan rituals eventually became secularized, and developed into children's games. They were probably brought to America by immigrants, particularly the Irish in the late nineteenth century. A treat is asked for or a trick is played. Bags of sweets and cookies are quite acceptable and if not forthcoming the wicked witches' curse will descend upon the house and its unfortunate occupants. The evening usually ends with ghost stories around a bonfire and mugs of hot pumpkin soup.

Pumpkin Soup

serves 8–10

Pumpkins were introduced to the early settlers by Indian tribes and are traditionally made into pies and soups. This is a beautiful-coloured soup.

1 large orange pumpkin
   1kg/2¼lb piece of pumpkin, cut into chunks
   1 medium onion, finely chopped
    small bunch of spring onions, finely chopped
    3–4 celery leaves, finely chopped
   1 clove garlic, minced
85g/3oz/⅓ cup butter
1.6litres/2¾pints/7cups chicken stock
350ml/12fl oz/1½cups single cream
20ml/1tablespoon/1½tablespoons chopped parsley
225g/8oz/3cups croûtons
salt and freshly ground black pepper

1 Slice the top off the pumpkin to make a lid, scrape out the seeds and stringy bits and carefully scoop out 1kg/2¼lb of flesh for the soup. (Use a separate piece of pumpkin if you prefer.)
2 Sauté the onion, spring onions, celery leaves and garlic in 50ml/3tablespoons/¼cup of the butter until tender but not brown.
3 Add the pumpkin chunks and cook gently for 10 minutes. Add the stock and simmer, stirring until the pumpkin is tender, about 15 minutes.
4 Remove from the heat and purée until smooth. Return to the pan, whisk in the cream and remaining butter and heat thoroughly without boiling. It should be satin smooth. Add salt and pepper to taste.
5 Warm the hollowed-out pumpkin in a preheated oven, 180°C/350°F/gas4, for 15 minutes. Pour in the hot soup, sprinkle with parsley and serve the croûtons separately.

Picking Piñon Nuts

Piñon (or pine) nuts are gathered in November around Santa Fe. According to local custom, everyone enjoys an energetic day out in the crisp air trooping into the mountains to the piñon and juniper forests to harvest the tiny nuts, which are found in the hard central core of the pine cones and can be notoriously difficult to crack open.

Unless carefully stored – preferably in the freezer – piñon nuts go rancid very quickly. New Mexicans use them throughout the year in breads, cookies, vegetable and meat dishes.

Spinach and Piñon Nuts

serves 4

This recipe is from Spanish colonial days and can also be made with Swiss chard or dandelion leaves or any combination of the three. The result has an earthy flavour that goes well with grilled meat and game.

550g/1½lb leaf spinach, washed
50ml/3tablespoons/¼cup olive oil
20g/1tablespoon/1½tablespoons piñon nuts
30g/1½tablespoons/2tablespoons raisins
2 garlic cloves, minced
pinch of cayenne
salt and freshly ground pepper

1 Put the spinach in a deep saucepan, cover and cook for about 5 minutes or until tender. Drain thoroughly and chop coarsely.
2 Heat the oil in a heavy frying-pan, add the nuts, raisins and the garlic. Sauté gently until the nuts and the garlic begin to colour. Do not let them burn.
3 Add the cooked spinach and heat through until the oil is absorbed. If it seems too dry, add a bit more oil.
4 Season with salt, pepper and cayenne to taste.

Feast Day Cookies

makes about 4 dozen

The Pueblo Indians make these crisp cookies for
Feast Days and celebrations. The cookies keep well
in an airtight tin and are wonderful dipped in
hot coffee.

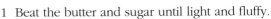

225g/8oz/1cup
   unsalted butter
115g/4oz/½cup
   sugar
140g/5oz/1cup
   wholemeal flour
285g/10oz/2cups
   self-raising flour
5ml/1teaspoon baking
   powder
pinch of salt
100g/3½oz/¼cup piñon nuts
100ml/4fl oz/½cup water
50ml/3tablespoons/¼cup sugar
5ml/1teaspoon cinnamon

1 Beat the butter and sugar until light and fluffy.
2 Combine the wholemeal flour, self-raising flour,
baking powder and salt, and gradually incorporate
into the butter and sugar, beating well.
3 Mix in the nuts and stir in the water gradually, to
form a stiff non-sticky dough. Wrap the dough in
cling film and chill for 30 minutes.
4 On a floured surface roll the dough 1cm/½in thick.
Cut into rounds 2.5cm/1½in in diameter.
5 Blend the sugar and the cinnamon and coat each
cookie. Arrange on baking sheets and cook in a
preheated oven, 190°C/375°F/gas5, for 15–20 minutes
or until the edges are just turning brown and the
cookies are pale golden. Cool on racks. The cookies
crisp up as they cool.

College Football Picnic

This is serious sport. During the fall semester the big game of the season against the traditional rival university very often falls on Homecoming weekend, when alumni make pilgrimages of thousands of miles to cheer on their team.

Fuelling this fervour demands warming food and drink. At the big games in the North-east, tailgate picnics served from the backs of station wagons are likely to include thermoses of stiff drink to insulate the fans from the bitter cold, and a good chocolate cake to take up the slack.

Bullshots

serves 1
Bullshots are best served hot and peppery, and kept handy in the family thermos.

100ml/4fl oz/½cup strong beef consommé
50ml/3tablespoons/¼cup vodka
salt and freshly ground pepper

1 Heat the consommé in a saucepan. When it is just about to boil remove from the heat, add the vodka, salt and pepper, stir and pour into a thermos.

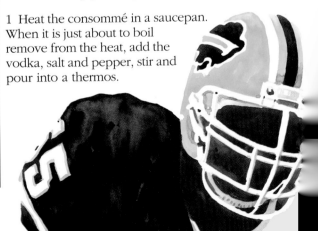

Crazy Chocolate Cake

serves 8

Crazy cake is mixed, baked, iced and transported to the picnic all in the same tin. The ingredients and the method may seem a bit unusual but it really works.

225g/8oz/1½cups self-raising flour
50ml/3tablespoons/¼cup cocoa powder
5ml/1teaspoon bicarbonate of soda
225g/8oz/1cup sugar
pinch of salt
75ml/5tablespoons/⅓cup sunflower oil
20ml/1tablespoon/1½tablespoons cider vinegar
5ml/1teaspoon vanilla extract
250ml/⅓pint/1cup cold water

Topping
115g/4oz/½cup unsalted butter, softened
115g/4oz/½cup brown sugar
30ml/1½tablespoons/2tablespoons double cream
75g/2½oz/½cup walnuts, coarsely chopped

1 Sift the flour, cocoa, soda, sugar and salt directly into a greased 20x20x5cm/9x9x2in cake tin.
2 Make three egg-sized depressions in the dry mixture; into one pour the oil, into the next the vinegar, and into the third the vanilla. Pour the water over the top and beat with a wooden spoon until almost smooth and the flour is incorporated.
3 Bake in a preheated oven, 180°C/350°F/gas4, for 30–35 minutes. Remove and cool in the tin for 10 minutes, but do not turn off the oven.
4 To make the topping, beat the butter, sugar and cream to a thick paste; spread on top of the warm cake, scatter over the walnuts and return to the oven for 3 minutes.
5 Leave to cool. Cut into squares and serve straight from the tin.

Thanksgiving Day

The Pilgrim Fathers, who braved the sea crossing in the seventeenth century from England to the New World, were better sailors than farmers. The seeds and plants they brought with them did not flourish in the harsh climate of what is now New England. Had the local Indian tribes not offered shelter from the bitter winter, and help with the spring planting of native crops, the Pilgrims would have perished. But, after that first successful harvest, they celebrated with a feast of Thanksgiving, and it was to the Indians as well as to the Lord that they gave thanks.

Thanksgiving, on the last Thursday in November, is celebrated in New York with a colourful parade along Central Park West. My family lived right on the route and there was always a breakfast party for family and friends who came to cheer the marchers from the wide balcony; enough molasses-gingernut muffins and hot chocolate to keep us cheering but not too much to spoil the evening feast. Our favourite 'trimmings' with the turkey were a traditional cornbread stuffing and a cranberry-onion conserve made by my Italian grandmother.

Cornbread Stuffing for a Turkey

enough to fill the cavity of a 5.5kg/12lb bird for traditional Thanksgiving dinner

115g/4oz/½cup butter, diced
500g/1lb corn bread, crumbled
280g/10oz/4cups soft breadcrumbs, white or whole-meal
115g/4oz/½cup bacon dripping or butter
150g/5½oz/1cup walnuts, chopped (optional)
125g/4½oz/1cup celery, diced
1 medium onion, finely chopped
1 green pepper, deseeded and finely chopped
10ml/2teaspoons salt
2.5ml/½teaspoon each of thyme, marjoram and sage
small bunch of parsley, chopped
2 large eggs, beaten
250–600ml/⅓–1pint/1–2cups turkey (or chicken) stock
freshly ground black pepper

1 Mix the butter, corn bread and breadcrumbs in a large bowl.
2 Heat the dripping or butter in a frying-pan, add the nuts (if used), celery, onion and green pepper and sauté slowly for 5 minutes.
3 Add to the corn bread mixture with the salt, pepper and herbs, mixing thoroughly.
4 Add the eggs and gradually mix in the stock, stirring gently until the stuffing is of the desired consistency, and not too sloppy.
5 Stuff lightly in the neck and body cavity of the turkey. If there is any left over spread it in a greased ovenproof gratin dish and bake for 30 minutes or until crisp on top.

Cranberry-Onion Conserve

makes about l litre/1¾ pints

A delicious alternative to the usual cranberry sauce, this conserve is excellent with game and terrines as well as the inevitable cold turkey.

60ml/3½tablespoons/¼cup + 2 teaspoons olive oil
900g/2lb sweet onions, thinly sliced
8 garlic cloves, minced
50ml/3tablespoons/¼cup cider vinegar
50ml/3tablespoons/¼cup brown sugar
450g/1lb cranberries
salt and freshly ground pepper to taste

1 Heat the oil in a wide, deep frying-pan, add the onions and the garlic and cook on a high heat, without stirring, for 5 minutes. Stir the onions and continue cooking, on medium heat, stirring occasionally to prevent burning, until they reach a deep glossy brown.

2 Add the vinegar, the brown sugar and the cranberries. Stir well and continue cooking on medium heat until the cranberries have dissolved, the mixture is thick, surplus liquid from the onions and the cranberries has evaporated and the fruit is soft. Add salt and pepper to taste.

3 Pack in clean, warm jars, seal and keep in the refrigerator for up to three months.

Molasses-Gingernut Muffins

makes about 24

For tender, light muffins, carefully stir rather than beat the mixture. You can also make this into a wonderful ginger cake, in which case you will need to use a well greased loose-bottomed 25cm/10in cake tin.

225g/8oz/1cup unsalted butter
350g/12oz/1cup molasses/treacle
1 large egg
170g/6oz/¾cup sugar
285g/10oz/2¼cups self-raising flour
5ml/1teaspoon bicarbonate of soda
10ml/2teaspoons ground ginger
5ml/1teaspoon cinnamon
2.5ml/½teaspoon grated nutmeg
pinch of ground cloves
grated rind of 1 orange
75g/2½oz/½cup walnuts, coarsely chopped
75g/2½oz/¼cup preserved ginger in syrup, drained
   and chopped
115ml/4fl oz/½cup boiling water
75ml/5tablespoons/⅓cup milk

1 Melt the butter with the molasses in a small saucepan and set aside to cool.
2 Beat the egg and sugar until light and fluffy.
3 Sift the flour, bicarbonate of soda and spices and add to the egg mixture, alternating with the molasses and butter mixture.
4 Fold in the orange rind, walnuts and ginger. Stir in the water and milk.
5 Butter muffin- or bun-tins with 2cm/1in wells. Fill each tin two-thirds full. Bake in a 180°C/350°F/gas4 oven for 20–25 minutes until brown and risen.
6 Leave to cool for 15 minutes in the tins. Serve warm, split and buttered. These muffins keep well and can also be frozen and reheated.

Colonial Chocolate Christmas Pudding

serves 6

Dense, fruity steamed suet puddings were at one time quite usual in America. Early colonial manuscripts and receipt books gave instructions for hundreds of these sturdy confections, but after the middle of the nineteenth century they began to be replaced with lighter steamed sponge puddings.

One Old Guard family who can proudly trace its lineage to the Mayflower descendants, the Daughters of the American Revolution and the founders of the Naval Academy in Annapolis, Maryland, has served chocolate pudding at Christmas for as long as anyone can remember. The original receipt, from the 1840s, is still preserved with the family documents. Their chocolate pudding is as excellent today as it was in colonial days, and is still brought flaming to the table with a silver bowl of chilled Hard Sauce.

285g/10oz/2cups self-raising flour
170g/6oz/1cup dark brown sugar
50ml/3tablespoons/¼cup cocoa powder
5ml/1teaspoon bicarbonate of soda
250ml/⅓pint/1cup buttermilk (or sour cream)
50ml/3tablespoons/¼cup melted butter
50ml/3tablespoons/¼cup brandy

1 Mix the flour and the sugar in a bowl with your fingers to break up any lumps. Sift in the cocoa and soda.
2 Mix together the buttermilk and melted butter and stir gently into the flour.

3 Pour the mixture into a buttered 2-pint pudding basin. Cover with a double layer of pleated tin foil (the pleat will allow room for expansion). Secure the foil with string and tie a handle over the top for lifting.
4 Steam, on a trivet, in 5cm/2in of boiling water for 1 hour. Make sure you don't let the boiling water dry out; keep checking and top up if necessary.
5 Let the pudding stand in the basin for 10 minutes, then unmould onto a serving platter. Heat the brandy in a ladle, carefully set it aflame and pour it at once over the pudding as you bring it in.

Hard Sauce

115g/4oz/1cup unsalted butter, softened
50ml/3tablespoons/¼cup double cream
170g/6oz/1cup brown sugar
40ml/2tablespoons/2½tablespoons brandy

Beat the butter with the cream, adding the sugar a little at a time. When the mixture is light and fluffy, beat in the brandy until it is thoroughly absorbed. Serve chilled.